CONTENTS

COUNTING DOWN THE DINOSAURS

Dinosaurs were huge reptiles that lived **hundreds of millions** of years ago. They first appeared after a mass extinction made room on Earth for a reptile takeover.

NOT THE FIRST MASS EXTINCTION - OR THE LAST

So far, there have been **five mass extinctions** in Earth's history. **Three** of them affected the dinosaurs:

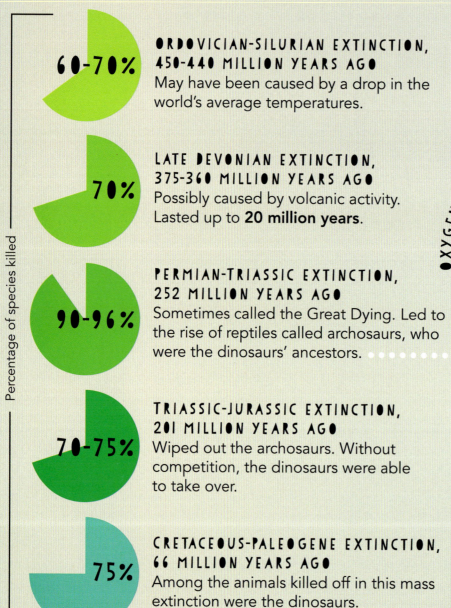

Percentage of species killed

60-70%

ORDOVICIAN-SILURIAN EXTINCTION, 450-440 MILLION YEARS AGO
May have been caused by a drop in the world's average temperatures.

70%

LATE DEVONIAN EXTINCTION, 375-360 MILLION YEARS AGO
Possibly caused by volcanic activity. Lasted up to **20 million years**.

90-96%

PERMIAN-TRIASSIC EXTINCTION, 252 MILLION YEARS AGO
Sometimes called the Great Dying. Led to the rise of reptiles called archosaurs, who were the dinosaurs' ancestors.

70-75%

TRIASSIC-JURASSIC EXTINCTION, 201 MILLION YEARS AGO
Wiped out the archosaurs. Without competition, the dinosaurs were able to take over.

75%

CRETACEOUS-PALEOGENE EXTINCTION, 66 MILLION YEARS AGO
Among the animals killed off in this mass extinction were the dinosaurs.

OXYGEN IN EARTH'S ATMOSPHERE

30%

Before this extinction, Earth's atmosphere was about **30% oxygen**. The oxygen level then fell to about **10%**. Oxygen levels have been rising ever since, to today's levels of about **21%**.

RISE OF THE ARCHOSAURS

After the Permian-Triassic extinction **252,000,000 years ago**, reptiles called archosaurs became the most dominant creatures on Earth. Archosaurs could be very different shapes and sizes, but had at least **two things** in common:

Archosaurs produced young from eggs.

Archosaurs all had **two 'extra' holes** on each side of their skull, as well as a nostril and an eye socket.

extra hole

eye socket

extra hole

nostril

WHAT MAKES A DINOSAUR A DINOSAUR?

Dinosaurs are descended from the archosaurs. The most noticeable feature of the dinosaurs was the way their legs worked.

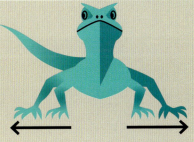

The early archosaurs walked with a wide stance, because their legs pointed outwards from their hips.

Dinosaurs walked with a narrower stance. Their legs went downwards from their hips.

Dinosaurs took over after the Triassic-Jurassic mass extinction killed off the archosaurs. Scientists are not sure why the dinosaurs survived while the archosaurs died out.

ARCHOSAUR DESCENDANTS

Dinosaurs were not the only archosaur descendants to survive the mass extinction. Others included crocodiles such as the giant Sarcosuchus, which even the fiercest predatory dinosaurs had to watch out for. Flying reptiles known as pterosaurs were also descended from the archosaurs.

DINOSAURS STALKED THE EARTH FOR 66 BILLION, 65 MILLION DAYS

Dinosaurs were around between about **247,000,000 and 66,000,000 million years ago**. That means dinosaurs were on Earth for **181,000,000 years** – which is **66.065 billion days**, or **1.58556 trillion hours**.

Compared to the dinosaurs, humans have only been on Earth for a very short time. The first humans appeared about **2,000,000 years ago**. Homo sapiens, our own species, has only been around for **200,000 years**.

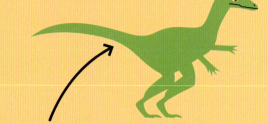

The oldest known dinosaur is Saltopus, from Scotland, which dates from **245,000,000 million years ago**.

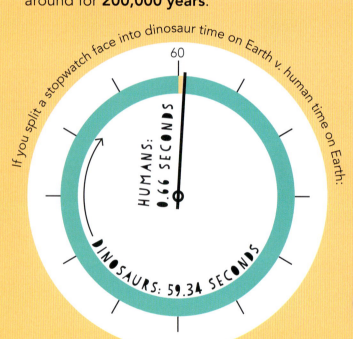

If you split a stopwatch face into dinosaur time on Earth v. human time on Earth:

60

HUMANS: 0.66 SECONDS

DINOSAURS: 59.34 SECONDS

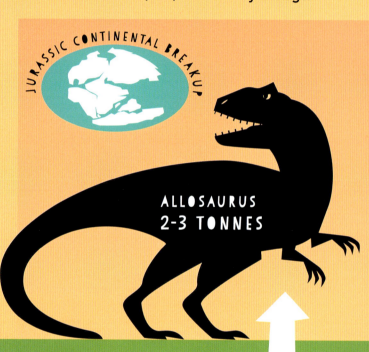

JURASSIC CONTINENTAL BREAKUP

ALLOSAURUS 2-3 TONNES

TRIASSIC PERIOD, 250-201 MILLION YEARS AGO

PANGAEA

At the start of the Triassic, Earth's land was joined in **one vast supercontinent** called Pangaea. The archosaurs dominated this period, but towards the end of it, large predatory dinosaurs such as Herrerasaurus and agile hunters like Liliensternus began to appear.

350 KG

HERRERASAURUS

THE JURASSIC PERIOD, 201-145 MILLION YEARS AGO

During the Jurassic period, Pangaea began to break up and the rise of the dinosaurs began. By the end of this period there was a wide range of them, including giant herbivores such as Brachiosaurus and armoured dinosaurs, such as Stegosaurus. Predators included Allosaurus and Ceratosaurus.

THE CRETACEOUS PERIOD, 145–66 MILLION YEARS AGO

During the Cretaceous period, Earth's continents began to slowly take shape. For their last **79 million years of existence**, dinosaurs were almost completely dominant. Carnivores such as Tyrannosaurus rex and Spinosaurus stalked the land. Huge herbivores such as Alamosaurus used their size as a defence, while smaller ones like Tarchia developed armoured skin.

CRETACEOUS CONTINENTAL BREAKUP

SPINOSAURUS
10 TONNES

TYRANNOSAURUS REX
6–8 TONNES

URSUS MARITIMUS
(POLAR BEAR)
1 TONNE

ROCKY REMAINS

We know about dinosaurs because of the remains, or fossils, they left behind. These fossils tell us what the dinosaurs were like, as well as when they lived.

The places where dinosaurs once lived are usually very different today. For example, dinosaur fossils have been found in the frozen Arctic – but back when dinosaurs lived there, this part of the world was warm and covered in plants.

Higher layers = younger fossils
Lower layers = older fossils

$8.36 MILLION COST OF A TYRANNOSAURUS REX IN 1997

Almost since dinosaur fossils were first discovered, people have been selling them. The value of the rarest and most interesting fossils has increased dramatically.

FAMOUS TYRANNOSAURUS REX

As well as being the most expensive, Sue (right) is probably the most famous Tyrannosaurus rex. Others include:

Tristan, visited by **millions of people a year** since going on display in the Naturkunde Museum in Berlin, Germany.

TRISTAN

Stan, who was found in the same Hell Creek formation as Sue and who now lives in the Black Hills Institute of Geological Research, USA.

TYRANNOSAURUS REX

1990
US$5,000
Paid in the USA for an almost-complete fossil of Tyrannosaurus rex, probably the most famous dinosaur.

EDMONTOSAURUS

2008
US$132,500
An almost-complete Edmontosaurus, a duck-billed dinosaur from the Cretaceous period.

LENGTH OF TEETH V. TIGER
Tyrannosaurus rex: up to **30 cm**

Tiger: up to **8 cm**

Considering how easy it is for a tiger to kill just about anything it meets (apart from another tiger), this makes Tyrannosaurus rex truly terrifying.

When the Naturkunde Museum in Berlin put Tristan on display in December 2014 the number of visitors leapt.

| 2014 | **463,000 visitors** |
| 2015 | **542,000 visitors** |

TRICERATOPS

2008
US$250,950
Popular and
unusual, a
Triceratops skull
cost almost
twice as much
as a whole
Edmontosaurus.

DIPLODOCUS

2013
US$652,0000
'Misty', as this
fossil was known,
was one of only
a few whole
Diplodocus
skeletons ever
found.

ALLOSAURUS AND STEGOSAURUS

2011
US$2,700,000
These **two fossils** were
unusual because they
were the remains of
dinosaurs that had died
fighting each other.

TYRANNOSAURUS REX

1997
US$8,362,500
The same dinosaur
as had been bought
for **US$5,000** in 1990
was sold **seven years
later** at an auction in
New York. Now named
Sue, it fetched **1,672.5
times as much.**

US$8,362,500

SPEED V. RUNNING HUMAN
Tyrannosaurus rex: **29 kph**
Terrified human: **26 kph**
The human's only hope would be to keep zigzagging until
Tyrannosaurus rex got tired – it could not keep up its top speed for long.

HELP!

THE WEIGHT OF THE HEAVIEST DINOSAUR WAS 80,000 KG

The hefty Argentinosaurus was a peaceful plant-eater rather than a predator. It lived in South America, along with other giants such as Patagotitan and Puertasaurus.

ARGENTINOSAURUS WEIGHED ABOUT THE SAME AS:

 1.1 space shuttles

10.5 elephants

13 Tyrannosaurus rex

 20 hippos

 1,000 men

Argentinosaurus probably weighed about **80 tonnes**, although palaeontologists do not agree on this. Some believe Argentinosaurus weighed around **60 tonnes**, others think it may have been as much as **100 tonnes**.

WEIGHT ESTIMATES

Estimating exactly how much any dinosaur weighed is tricky when you have only fossils to work from. It gets more difficult as the dinosaurs get bigger, too.

For example, experts say that the raptor Deinonychus weighed between **60 kg** and **75 kg**. An extra **15 kg** does not sound like much: it's only the same as about **two dachshunds**. But **15 kg** is **25%** of **60 kg**. Applying the same increase to other dinosaurs can have a much bigger effect, as the examples on the right show.

An extra **20 tonnes** is the same weight as about **three Tyrannosaurus rex**, or **40 grizzly bears**.

TITANOSAURS

Argentinosaurus was a titanosaur. The titanosaurs had large bodies, long necks and tails, and small heads. They lived almost everywhere during the late Cretaceous period, but died out with the other dinosaurs **66 million years ago**.

TRICERATOPS

For Triceratops, an extra **25%** means adding the weight of a large rhinoceros.

•11.25 TONNES
9 TONNES

7.5 TONNES
6 TONNES

TYRANNOSAURUS REX

For one of the biggest predatory dinosaurs, **25% extra** adds about the same weight as a car.

MICRORAPTOR

750 G
600 G

For the smallest dinosaur, **25% extra weight** adds only about **three-quarters of a hamster.**

WHY WERE THE TITANOSAURS SO BIG?

No one is certain why the titanosaurs grew so big. Their size made them harder for predators to attack, so this may be **one reason**. Even Carcharodontosaurus, the huge predator that hunted Argentinosaurus, weighed **only a tenth as much**.

Saltasaurus

The titanosaurs had other ways to defend themselves, as well as their size. They seem to have lived in herds, protecting themselves through numbers like modern-day wildebeest. Some titanosaurs had skin toughened with hard scales and one, Saltasaurus, even had bony plates like an ankylosaur.

11

1,000 TEETH LINED THE JAWS OF NIGERSAURUS

Nigersaurus was a **two-tonne** plant-eater from Niger, in Africa. Like other dinosaurs, its teeth were replaced as they wore out – but no other dinosaur had quite as many teeth as Nigersaurus.

Nigersaurus needed all those teeth because of its diet which was mainly tough plants that grew at ground level.

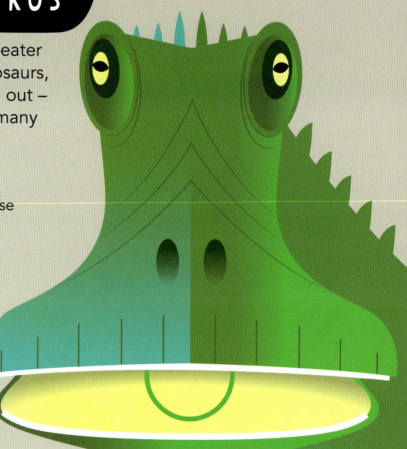

TO FIT THEM INTO ITS MOUTH, NIGERSAURUS HAD A FEW SPECIAL ADAPTATIONS:

1. Its teeth were very small, just a few millimetres across.

2. They were arranged in rows, with **8–10 teeth** in each row.

3. The teeth were very tightly packed together, with no gaps between them.

4. Nigersaurus had a jaw that was wider than it was deep.

It must have been like a huge, toothy lawnmower, clearing strips of vegetation as it chomped its way along!

NIGERSAURUS TOOTH LOSS

Each of Nigersaurus's teeth may only have lasted **2–3 weeks** before being pushed out by a replacement from behind. Assuming each tooth lasted **17.5 days**, Nigersaurus would have used up a LOT of teeth:

Per day:	**57 teeth**
Per week:	**400 teeth**
Per month:	**1,714 teeth**
Per year:	**20,857 teeth**

TYPICAL NUMBER OF TEETH IN FULLY GROWN ADULTS.

Nigersaurus **1,000**

Spinosaurus* **64**

Tyrannosaurus rex* **60**

Great white shark* **48**

Alsatian dog **42**

Cow **32**

Human **32**

Tiger **30**

DINOSAUR TEETH

In areas where fossils are common, such as the Jurassic Coast in southern England, fossil hunters regularly unearth dinosaur teeth. We can tell a lot about dinosaurs from their teeth and jaws. Nigersaurus's tiny teeth and super-wide jaw suited its plant-eating diet, and other dinosaurs also had teeth that were adapted to their diets.

*These animals also had/have other teeth developing. Great white sharks, for example, have **48 teeth** on the front line – but about **240 more** growing inside their jaw.

TYRANNOSAURUS REX (CARNIVORE)
Length: **30 cm**
Pointed, conical teeth designed for biting into prey, then ripping out chunks of flesh.

SPINOSAURUS (CARNIVORE)
Length: **25 cm**
Spinosaurus was mainly a fish-eater and its long, sharp teeth were perfect for keeping hold of wriggling, slippery fish.

CARCHARODONTOSAURUS (CARNIVORE)
Length: **25 cm**
Carcharodontosaurus had curving, pointed teeth with a serrated edge like a bread knife for slashing through flesh.

CAMARASAURUS (HERBIVORE)
Length: **19 cm**
Shaped like a thick spoon or a chisel, these teeth were strong and show that Camarasaurus ate tough plants.

TRICERATOPS (HERBIVORE)
Length: **4 cm**
Triceratops teeth are common fossils because so many were worn down and spat out. Triceratops' teeth were designed for grinding up large amounts of plant matter.

VELOCIRAPTOR (CARNIVORE)
Length: 2 cm
Teeth were not Velociraptor's main weapon. Like all raptors, it used the sickle claw on its feet for attacking victims, and its arms for gripping on to them.

800 SPECIES OF DINOSAUR STILL TO BE DISCOVERED

At the moment, we know of about **500–600 different species of dinosaur**. This does not seem like many for an animal that ruled the Earth for almost **200,000,000 years**.

FOSSILS

We learn about dinosaurs through their fossils. These were formed after dinosaurs died. Dead creatures do not usually form fossils: their bodies simply decay over time and disappear. Fossils only form under particular circumstances, for example:

1. A sea creature dies and sinks to the bottom.

2. It is covered in mud and does not rot away.

3. Over time it becomes rock.

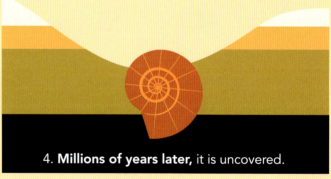

4. **Millions of years later,** it is uncovered.

Some dinosaur species may never have been fossilised. Others may have become fossils so rarely that they have not yet been discovered. There may also be fossil-rich layers of rock far below Earth's surface, where we cannot yet reach them.

THE BONANZA EFFECT

The 'bonanza effect' is when you look for something where it has been found before. So, fossil-hunters often look for fossils where someone has already uncovered some. This means fossil-hunting tends to happen in specific places. There could be many fossils of new species elsewhere.

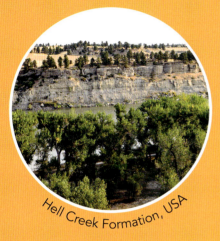

Hell Creek Formation, USA

The Hell Creek rock formation in the USA has produced many fossils.

- Triceratops
- Tyrannosaurus rex
- Edmontosaurus
- Thescelosaurus
- Ornithomimus
- Pachycephalosaurus
- Ankylosaurus

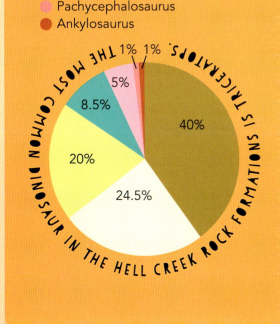

THE MOST COMMON DINOSAUR IN THE HELL CREEK ROCK FORMATIONS IS TRICERATOPS.

40%
24.5%
20%
8.5%
5%
1%
1%

UNDISCOVERED DINOSAURS

Experts have worked out that once you account for the rarity of fossils, the numbers that are still buried deep underground and the bonanza effect, there are probably at least **800 dinosaur species** still to be discovered.

We have so far only uncovered about **40% of the dinosaurs** that once walked the Earth.

RECLASSIFICATION

Dinosaurs are sometimes reclassified. This happens if palaeontologists decide that a fossil they thought was a separate species actually belongs to **one** they had already named (or the other way round). One example of this is the story of Brontosaurus:

1879
US palaeontologist Othniel Charles Marsh decides to call **one** of the new dinosaurs he has just discovered Brontosaurus.
Number of species: **+1**

1903
It is decided that Brontosaurus is actually so similar to Apatosaurus that they are the same species. Because Apatosaurus had been named first (in 1877), Brontosaurus loses its name.
Number of species: **-1**

2015
A new study decides there are too many differences between the **two fossils** for them to be the same species. Brontosaurus is back!
Number of species: **+1**

540 SPECIES OF DINOSAUR THAT HAVE BEEN NAMED

Once a new kind of dinosaur has been discovered, it is given a name. A dinosaur's name is often in **two parts** – for example, Tyrannosaurus rex.

The name tells you the dinosaur's species.

TYRANNOSAURUS REX MEANS 'KING OF THE TYRANT LIZARDS'.

Every animal in a species is almost the same, with only small differences such as height or skin patterns. Animals from the same species can have young together.

NEXT STOP, GENUS

Similar dinosaur species are grouped together in a 'genus'. The species in a genus share a lot of features, but are not exactly alike. The genus Tyrannosaurus, for example, does not just contain Tyrannosaurus rex. There are also at least **three other Tyrannosaurus species.**

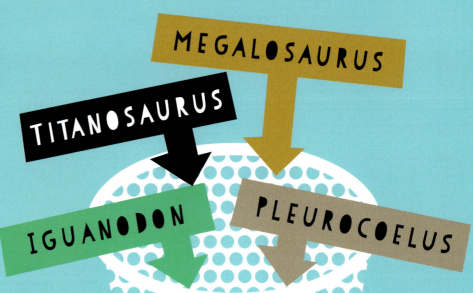

MEGALOSAURUS

TITANOSAURUS

IGUANODON

PLEUROCOELUS

INTO THE WASTEBASKET

Sometimes dinosaurs are put into a genus because palaeontologists are not sure where else to put them. These are known as 'wastebasket taxons'.

Some of the dinosaur wastebasket taxons

DINOSAUR FAMILIES

A 'family' is a group of dinosaurs whose genera (more than one genus) are similar, but not quite the same. For example, Tyrannosaurus is part of the tyrannosaur family, which also includes the Albertosaurus genus and Gorgosaurus genus.

DINOSAUR ORDERS

Every dinosaur belongs to one of **two 'orders':** saurischian or ornithischian. Ornithischian dinosaurs had hips like those of today's birds. Saurischians had hips like a modern lizard's.

The orders are divided into sub-orders, according to each dinosaur's special features. For example, **one of the sub-orders** of saurischian dinosaurs is the theropods. All theropods had hollow bones, **three-toed feet** and meat-eating ancestors.

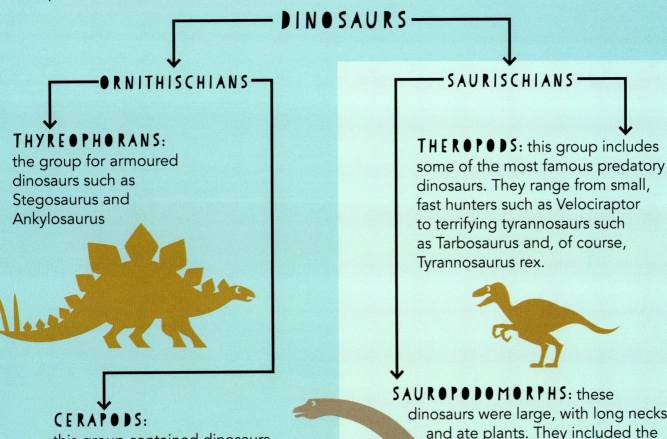

DINOSAURS

ORNITHISCHIANS

THYREOPHORANS: the group for armoured dinosaurs such as Stegosaurus and Ankylosaurus

CERAPODS: this group contained dinosaurs with thickened, fringed or horned heads, such as Pachycephalosaurus, Triceratops and Parasaurolophus.

SAURISCHIANS

THEROPODS: this group includes some of the most famous predatory dinosaurs. They range from small, fast hunters such as Velociraptor to terrifying tyrannosaurs such as Tarbosaurus and, of course, Tyrannosaurus rex.

SAUROPODOMORPHS: these dinosaurs were large, with long necks, and ate plants. They included the biggest land animals ever, the giants Argentinosaurus and Diplodocus.

17

64 KPH SPEED OF THE FASTEST DINOSAUR

Most of the fastest land dinosaurs were ostrich-like ones that ran on their back legs.

COMPSOGNATHUS: 64 kph, Europe, **150 million years ago**

DINOSAUR RACE

Working out the top speeds of animals that have been dead for **66 million years** is not easy, so these are estimates:

USAIN BOLT: **44.72 kph**, 2009

The fastest dinosaur was **144%** faster than Usain Bolt.

COMPSOGNATHUS: *top speed 64 kph*

A study of predatory dinosaurs in 2007 claimed that Compsognathus, a small dinosaur about the size of a turkey, may have been able to reach **64 kph**.

ORNITHOMIMUS: *top speed 60 kph*

The lower half of its legs (the tibia) was **20% longer** than the upper half (the femur) – just like in modern speedsters such as the cheetah.

VELOCIRAPTOR: *top speed 39 kph*

Its name means 'speedy thief', but Velociraptor was no match for the ornithomimosaurs. Even so, it was a lot faster than some of the dinosaurs it hunted, such as Protoceratops.

ALLOSAURS, TYRANNOSAURS: *top speed 34 kph*

The fastest of these was probably Allosaurus, which was about **5 kph** faster than Tyrannosaurus rex. The tyrannosaurs could not keep up their top speed for long, so they relied on sudden attacks.

ARGENTINOSAURUS and other giant sauropods: *top speed 8–12 kph*

With such a low top speed, just about any predator could catch up with these super-sized beasts. The challenge was how to attack once they did!

THE FASTEST DINOSAURS WOULD HAVE FOUND IT EASY TO SMASH THE WORLD 100-M RECORD:

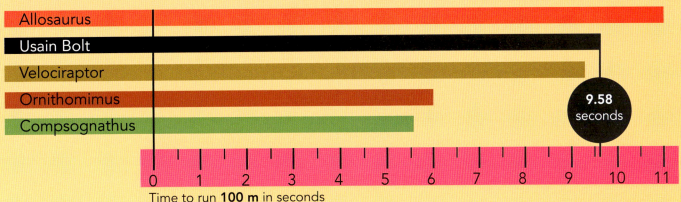

Allosaurus	
Usain Bolt	**9.58** seconds
Velociraptor	
Ornithomimus	
Compsognathus	

0 1 2 3 4 5 6 7 8 9 10 11

Time to run **100 m** in seconds

*The dinosaurs' times assume they could travel at top speed the whole way. If Bolt had done this, his **100-m record** would be **8.05 seconds**.

FAST-FLYING RIVALS

The ornithomimosaurs had a rival for the fastest-moving creatures around: the pterosaurs. Pterosaurs were not dinosaurs; they were flying reptiles. On land, pterosaurs such as Quetzalcoatlus walked on the 'elbows' of their folded-back wings. Once airborne, they may have travelled on the wind at up to **130 kph** – fast enough to fly from London to Moscow in under **23 hours**.

FEATHERED NON-FLYERS

Ornithomimus is one of the dinosaurs palaeontologists know had feathers on its arms/wings. These feathers would have been no good for flying.

Experts think that they might have been used for display, for example when finding a mate.

19

23 HOURS IN A DINOSAUR DAY

Days were an hour shorter during the dinosaurs' lifetime. The Earth spun more quickly, so it took less time before the Sun reappeared on the horizon.

PREHISTORIC TIME

As there were fewer hours in a day, hours, minutes and seconds were all slower in prehistoric times:

TODAY
24 hours

PREHISTORIC TIME
23 hours

1 DAY

TODAY: 60 minutes

PREHISTORIC TIME: 57.5 minutes

1 HOUR

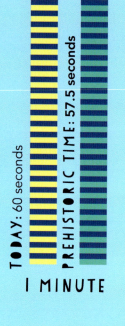

TODAY: 60 seconds

PREHISTORIC TIME: 57.5 seconds

1 MINUTE

TODAY: 1/60th of a minute

PREHISTORIC TIME: 0.9583 seconds

1 SECOND

EARTH ROTATES

The reason the Earth spins more slowly today, giving us longer days, is because of lunar gravity.

Moon pulls water towards it (a high tide)

Earth's rotation pulls the tidal bulge away, but the Moon's gravity pulls back. This pulling-back slows the Earth's rotation by a small amount every **million years or so**.

HOW DID DINOSAURS SLEEP?

We don't know much about how dinosaurs slept. Did they stand up, kneel, lie down? Tyrannosaurus rex had such tiny arms it wouldn't have been able to use them to push itself upright if it lay down. However, a few fossils of smaller dinosaurs have been found with them asleep, curled up like modern birds.

NIGHT-TIME DINOSAURS

Some dinosaurs were active at night. Scientists use the size of a dinosaur's eye socket and the scleral ring, part of the eye that is bigger in nocturnal animals, to work out if a dinosaur was nocturnal. They now know that the chance of meeting a Velociraptor, for example, was much higher at midnight than midday.

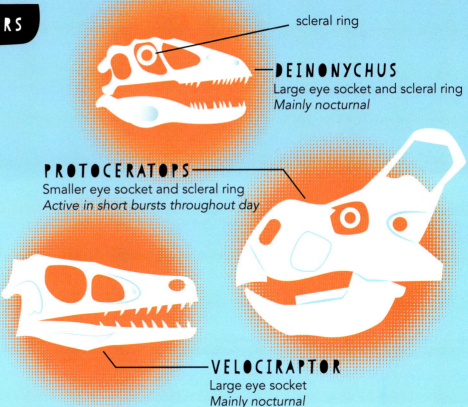

scleral ring

DEINONYCHUS
Large eye socket and scleral ring
Mainly nocturnal

PROTOCERATOPS
Smaller eye socket and scleral ring
Active in short bursts throughout day

VELOCIRAPTOR
Large eye socket
Mainly nocturnal

F-NUMBER EYES

Scientists use a number called an 'f number' to show how good an eye is at letting in light. Lower numbers are given to the eyes that let in more light. An f number of about **1** is a sign that an animal is active in the dark. A number about **2** shows it is active in light.

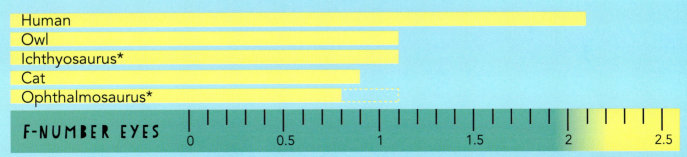

Human
Owl
Ichthyosaurus*
Cat
Ophthalmosaurus*

F-NUMBER EYES 0   0.5   1   1.5   2   2.5

*Ichthyosaurus and Ophthalmosaurus were ichthyosaurs, a type of marine animal from the age of dinosaurs.

NIGHT EYES?

As many of today's reptiles have slit pupils, dinosaurs often used to be drawn with slit pupils in their eyes. But birds, which are descended from dinosaurs, have round pupils, so many dinosaurs are now drawn like this. The dinosaurs that are most likely to have had slit pupils were the nocturnal dinosaurs, as this eye structure is often seen in animals with good night vision.

18 SPINES IN A SPINOSAURUS'S SAIL

Spinosaurus is probably the biggest predatory dinosaur discovered so far, at **around 17 m long**. This fish-eating monster hunted in rivers and estuaries. It is even more famous for the sail on its back than for its size.

No one is sure what Spinosaurus's sail was for, but there are **three main theories**:

SHOWING OFF
In this theory, the biggest (and perhaps most colourful) sail would be best. If a Spinosaurus was looking for a mate, it would choose the one with the best sail.

WARMING UP
As a fish-eater, Spinosaurus spent a lot of time in the water. If its sail was in the warm air, this could have warmed its blood and stopped it getting too cold.

STORING FAT
The **18 spines** are so strong some experts think they supported a hump, not a sail. It could have been used to store fat.

WAR DAMAGE

The first Spinosaurus fossils ever discovered were destroyed by bombs during the Second World War (1939–1945). They were in a museum in Munich, Germany, at the time. As they were also the only Spinosaurus fossils around at the time, this was a bit of a disaster.

1915 SPINOSAURUS

Spinosaurus was first discovered in 1915, when the most important bones found included:

 **20 TEETH**

13 BACKBONES

 9 SPINES

5 JAWBONES

It was almost **100 years** before another big Spinosaurus was discovered in 2014.

DINOSAUR BONES

Finding a fossilised dinosaur bone is not that easy – especially for rare dinosaurs such as Spinosaurus. Finding the whole skeleton of any dinosaur is very unusual.

Most dinosaurs in museums are not based on complete skeletons. At least some of the bones are usually from other fossils, or are reconstructions of what scientists think they might have looked like.

90% REAL
Sue the Tyrannosaurus rex
Field Museum, Chicago, USA

Sophie the Stegosaurus has about **50 bones** just in its skull, and **360 bones** in its almost-complete skeleton.

85% REAL
Sophie the Stegosaurus
Natural History Museum, London, UK

75% REAL
Lane the Triceratops
Houston Museum for Natural Science, USA

A Tyrannosaurus rex had about **200 bones** in its entire body – about the same as a fully grown human.

8°C WARMER ON PLANET DINOSAUR THAN TODAY

When dinosaurs ruled the Earth, the world was a lot warmer than it is now. **8°C** does not sound much, but remember that during the last ice age it was 5–9°C colder than today – and that had a **BIG** effect.

TODAY: North American farmer rides on tractor

LAST ICE AGE: North American farmer would be buried under 1 km of snow and ice

ARCTIC WARMTH

It was so warm in dinosaur times that there was no permanent ice at the poles, and a few dinosaurs roamed even the coldest areas. The recently discovered hadrosaur Ugrunaaluk is thought to have been able to survive the dark Arctic winters, in temperatures of less than 6°C.

Ugrunaaluk was discovered in Alaska.

NORTH · LATITUDE · SOUTH

ARCTIC CIRCLE

40°

North America

EQUATOR   0°   23°C

40°

WORLD AS IT IS TODAY

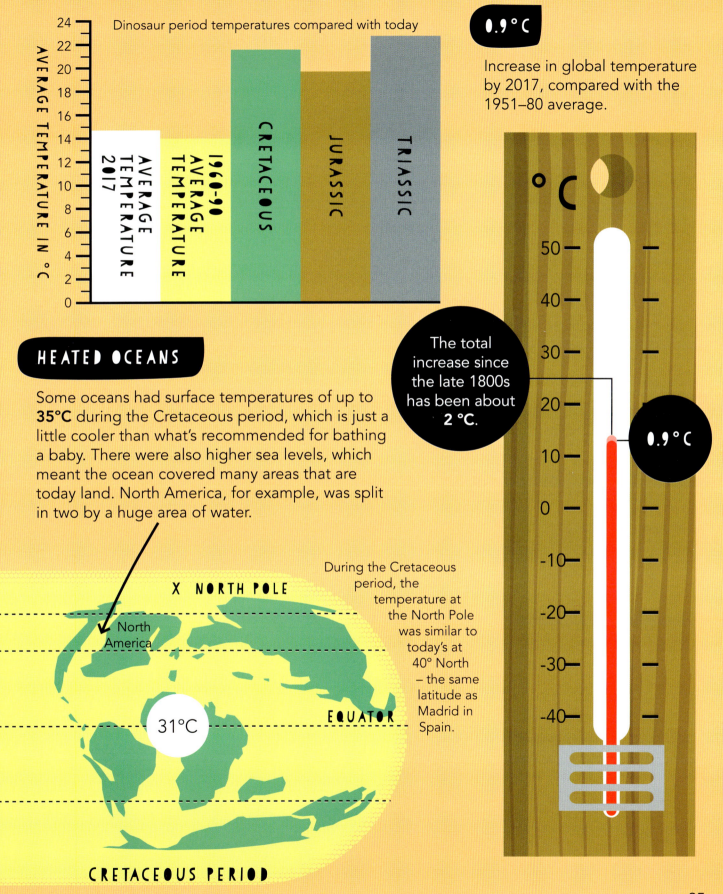

Dinosaur period temperatures compared with today

AVERAGE TEMPERATURE IN °C

24
22
20
18
16
14
12
10
8
6
4
2
0

AVERAGE TEMPERATURE 2017

1960–90 AVERAGE TEMPERATURE

CRETACEOUS

JURASSIC

TRIASSIC

0.9 °C

Increase in global temperature by 2017, compared with the 1951–80 average.

HEATED OCEANS

Some oceans had surface temperatures of up to **35°C** during the Cretaceous period, which is just a little cooler than what's recommended for bathing a baby. There were also higher sea levels, which meant the ocean covered many areas that are today land. North America, for example, was split in two by a huge area of water.

The total increase since the late 1800s has been about **2 °C**.

°C

50
40
30
20
10
0
-10
-20
-30
-40

0.9 °C

X NORTH POLE

North America

31°C

EQUATOR

During the Cretaceous period, the temperature at the North Pole was similar to today's at 40° North – the same latitude as Madrid in Spain.

CRETACEOUS PERIOD

TWO SEPARATE EVENTS WIPED OUT THE DINOSAURS

Scientists are not **100% certain** what killed the dinosaurs. Most, though, think it was a combination of **two events** that caused the world to change. The dinosaurs could not adapt quickly enough to survive.

ENORMOUS ERUPTIONS

Around the time the dinosaurs died out, a series of massive volcanic eruptions happened in India, forming what is now known as the Deccan Traps. They produced a layer of magma that today covers **2.6 million square km** and is up to **2.4 km thick**.

The Deccan Traps were formed around 66 million years ago.

DECCAN TRAPS

These eruptions produced **227 times as much material** as the catastrophic eruption of Mount Tambora in Indonesia in 1815.

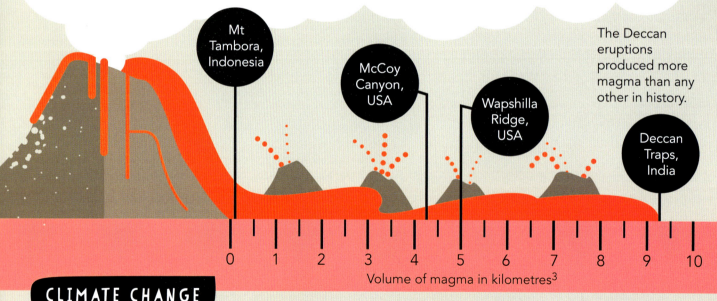

Mt Tambora, Indonesia

McCoy Canyon, USA

Wapshilla Ridge, USA

The Deccan eruptions produced more magma than any other in history.

Deccan Traps, India

0   1   2   3   4   5   6   7   8   9   10

Volume of magma in kilometres^3

CLIMATE CHANGE

The Deccan eruptions released gases into Earth's atmosphere, affecting the climate:
- Carbon dioxide began to trap heat in the Earth's atmosphere, increasing the temperature.
- Sulphur caused acid rain, which killed plants and affected the planet's water.

Both these effects began to have an impact on the dinosaurs. Some found it hard to survive in the changing temperatures. Others found they did not have enough to eat.

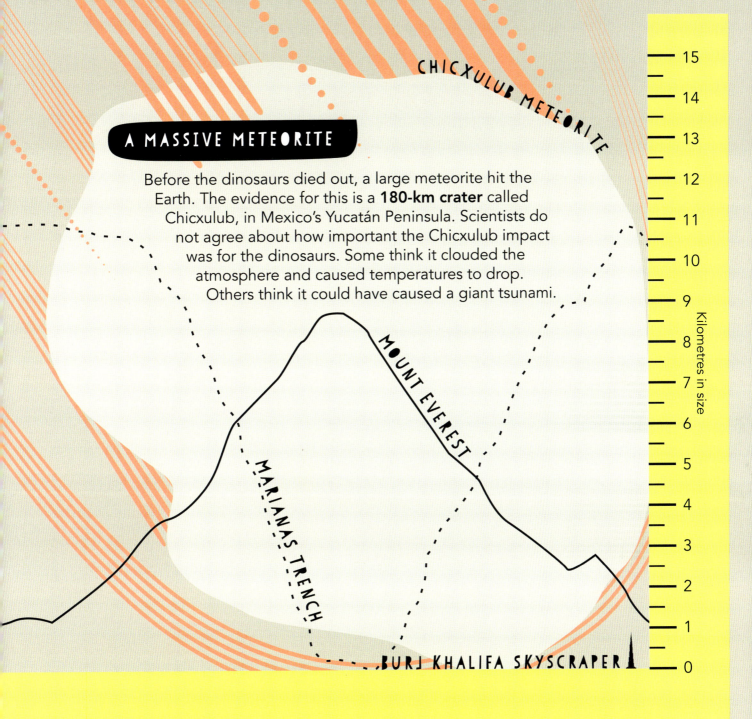

A MASSIVE METEORITE

Before the dinosaurs died out, a large meteorite hit the Earth. The evidence for this is a **180-km crater** called Chicxulub, in Mexico's Yucatán Peninsula. Scientists do not agree about how important the Chicxulub impact was for the dinosaurs. Some think it clouded the atmosphere and caused temperatures to drop. Others think it could have caused a giant tsunami.

CHICXULUB METEORITE

MOUNT EVEREST

MARIANAS TRENCH

BURJ KHALIFA SKYSCRAPER

Kilometres in size

15
14
13
12
11
10
9
8
7
6
5
4
3
2
1
0

DINOSAURS SURVIVE!

Although there are no longer any Tyrannosaurs roaming the American plains, or Tarchia trundling about in Mongolia, the dinosaurs did not completely die out. Most scientists agree that today's birds evolved from dinosaurs.

Every time you look a sparrow in the eye, you are face-to-face with a dinosaur descendant.

THE SMARTEST DINOSAUR WAS 1/10TH AS SMART AS A DOLPHIN

Experts think the smartest dinosaur was Troodon. Troodon was a small, birdlike dinosaur. Its brain was unusually big for such a small animal.

MEASURING DINOSAUR INTELLIGENCE

It is not easy to know how smart dinosaurs were. Experts use a measure called 'encephalisation quotient', or EQ. This measures the size of an animal's brain compared to its body.

- A small brain in a large body gives a low EQ. Once the animal has used brain power for breathing, seeing, hearing and smelling, it has little left for other activities.

- A large brain in a small body gives a high EQ. It suggests the animal will still have 'spare' brain power, once basic activities have been dealt with.

The least intelligent dinosaur of all is said to have been Stegosaurus. It had a brain only **3 cm long** – about the size of a walnut – though its body was as big as an elephant's.

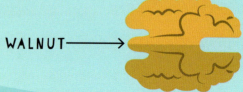
WALNUT ⟶

Actual size

HUMAN
5.0 EQ
12.8 x Troodon brain power

DOLPHIN
3.6 EQ
9.2 x Troodon brain power

RED COLOBUS MONKEY
1.5 EQ
3.8 x Troodon brain power

RELATIVE INTELLIGENCE

Herbivorous dinosaurs were not very intelligent (even compared to the other tiny-brained dinosaurs). The meat-eaters that hunted such animals – from Velociraptor to Tyrannosaurus rex – only had to be a tiny bit smarter than them to catch their prey.

BRAINS V. BITES

In general, a lot of the space in a dinosaur's skull was taken up by its jaw muscles. The brain was protected by a thick layer of bone, to keep it safe. No wonder there was little room left in a dinosaur's head for the brain itself!

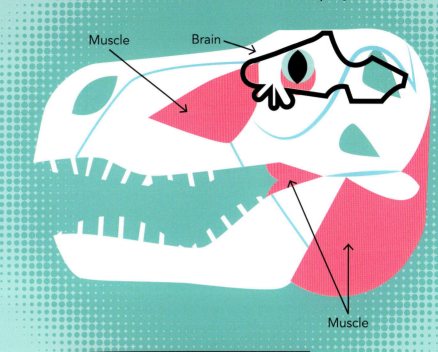

Muscle   Brain

Muscle

THE 'TWO BRAINS' MYTH

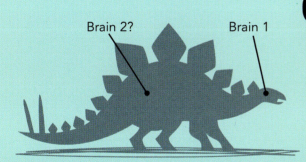

Brain 2?   Brain 1

Some dinosaurs – Stegosaurus and large sauropods such as Camarasaurus – were once thought to have had **two brains**. The **second** was thought to be in a large cavity in their spine, close to their hips. Scientists now know that this cavity did not contain the nerve cells that make up a brain. What they don't know is what WAS inside it.

TROODON
0.39 EQ
This makes Troodon about as smart as a chicken

TRICERATOPS
0.11 EQ
One-third the brain power of Troodon

BRACHIOSAURUS
Less than 0.1 EQ
Like other large sauropods, Brachiosaurus had about **one-quarter** the brain power of Troodon

FURTHER INFORMATION

BOOKS
Know It All: Dinosaurs by Andrew Langley (Franklin Watts, 2015)
Write On: Dinosaurs by Clare Hibbert (Franklin Watts, 2016)
The Science of...Prehistoric Giants, Killer Dinosaurs by Steve Parker and *Flying Reptiles* by Alex Woolf (Book House, 2017)
Dinosaur! (Dorling Kindersley, 2014)

WEBSITES
For photos, videos and news, head here and search 'dinosaurs':
www.natgeokids.com/uk/

To find out more about your favourite dinosaurs, including size comparisons to a fully grown human, click on the 'species' button here: **prehistoric-wildlife.com**
For games, videos, advice on how to draw dinosaurs and even an interview with a tyrannosaur go to: **www.amnh.org/explore/ology/paleontology**

Note to parents and teachers:
Every effort has been made by the publisher to ensure that these websites contain no inappropriate or offensive material. However, because of the nature of the Internet, it is impossible to guarantee that the content of these sites will not be altered. We strongly advise that Internet access is supervised by a responsible adult.

LARGE NUMBERS

1,000,000,000,000,000,000,000,000,000,000,000 = ONE DECILLION
1,000,000,000,000,000,000,000,000,000,000 = ONE NONILLION
1,000,000,000,000,000,000,000,000,000 = ONE OCTILLION
1,000,000,000,000,000,000,000,000 = ONE SEPTILLION
1,000,000,000,000,000,000,000 = ONE SEXTILLION
1,000,000,000,000,000,000 = ONE QUINTILLION
1,000,000,000,000,000 = ONE QUADRILLION
1,000,000,000,000 = ONE TRILLION
1,000,000,000 = ONE BILLION
1,000,000 = ONE MILLION
1000 = ONE THOUSAND
100 = ONE HUNDRED
10 = TEN
1 = ONE

GLOSSARY

acid rain	rain that has a higher-than-normal amount of the chemicals sulphur dioxide and nitrogen oxide in it. These chemicals make the rain acidic, harming forests and lakes
anatomy	science of the physical structure of animals and humans, especially their bones and muscles
ankylosaur	one of a group of dinosaurs that were protected by bony armour, with large plates (called osteoderms) on their heads, backs and tails
carnivore	animal that eats mostly or entirely meat
cavity	hollow space inside a hard structure such as bone or rock
climate	the typical weather and temperature of a place, measured over a long period of time
crater	big, bowl-shaped hole in the ground, caused by a meteorite or a volcanic eruption
estuary	place where a river and the sea meet, and the water becomes salty at high tide
evolve	change and improve. Living things evolve because the ones that are best at surviving in their environment have most chance of surviving and producing young
extinction	complete disappearance of a species of living thing
eye socket	part of the skull that holds an animal's eyeball
gravity	force of attraction that pulls all objects together. Larger objects have stronger gravity
hadrosaur	one of a group of plant-eating dinosaurs that had duck-like mouths
herbivore	animal that eats only plants
ice age	period of time when the temperature is low and large areas of land are always covered in thick ice. The last ice age ended 11,700 years ago
lunar	to do with the Moon
magma	hot fluid – usually molten rock – from beneath the Earth's crust. Magma usually forms lava when it reaches the surface
mate	animal of the opposite sex with which to have young
meteorite	piece of rock or metal that has fallen to Earth from space
nocturnal	awake and feeding mostly at night
palaeontologist	scientist who studies fossilised plants and animals
petrified	preserved by being turned to stone
poles	northernmost and southernmost parts of Earth
pupil	centre part of an eye, which can gets larger or smaller to let in different amounts of light
raptor	member of a group of dinosaurs that had an extra-long claw on their foot. The claw was a raptor's main weapon, and was used to slash at prey
serrated	with a wavy edge, like a knife for cutting bread
skeleton	bony structure that supports an animal's body
species	member of a group of animals or plants that are very similar. Members of the same species are able to have young together
spine	backbone, the line of bones protecting nerves that carry signals from and to the brain
stance	how an animal stands. For example, if you stand with your feet far apart you have a wide stance. Feet together, you have a narrow stance
taxon	word used to group living things into different classifications
tsunami	large wave caused by movement of the Earth's crust or volcanic activity

INDEX